ANGINA DAYS | SELECTED POEMS

FACING PAGES **FACING PAGES**

NICHOLAS JENKINS

Series Editor

ANGINA DAYS | SELECTED POEMS

Günter Eich

Translated and Introduced by Michael Hofmann

PRINCETON UNIVERSITY PRESS

Princeton and Oxford

Requests for permission to reproduce material from this work should be sent to
Permissions, Princeton University Press

German poems were selected from, *Gesammelte Werke* by Günter Eich,
copyright © 1991 Suhrkamp Verlag, Frankfurt am Main, and used by
permission of Suhrkamp Verlag.

Published by Princeton University Press, 41 William Street, Princeton,
New Jersey 08540

In the United Kingdom: Princeton University Press, 6 Oxford Street,
Woodstock, Oxfordshire OX20 1TW

LIBRARY OF CONGRESS CATALOGING-IN-PUBLICATION DATA
Eich, Günter, 1907–1972.
  [Poems. English & German. Selections]
  Gunter Eich : selected poems / translated by Michael Hofmann.
      p. cm. — (Facing pages)
  ISBN 978-0-691-14497-9 (acid-free paper)   1. Eich, Günter, 1907–1972—Translations
into English.   I. Hofmann, Michael, 1957 Aug. 25–   II. Title.
  PT2609.I17A2 2010

      831'.914—dc22   2009039559

British Library Cataloging-in-Publication Data is available

This book has been composed in Minion

Printed on acid-free paper. ∞

press.princeton.edu

Printed in the United States of America

10   9   8   7   6   5   4   3   2   1

For Curtis D'Costa

CONTENTS

from *Zu den Akten / Ad Acta* (1964)

from *Anlässe und Steingärten / Occasions and Rock Gardens* (1966)

ACKNOWLEDGMENTS

Some of these translations first appeared in the anthology *Twentieth Century German Poetry* (Farrar, Straus and Giroux, 2006) and in the journals *Common Knowledge*, *Kenyon Review*, the *London Review of Books*, the *New York Review of Books*, *Poetry* (Chicago), and *Threepenny Review* to whose editors—where appropriate—grateful acknowledgment is made. Further thanks are owing to Petra Hardt, of the Suhrkamp Verlag, for her support of the project, and to my onetime *Tischnachbar* and later friend (we were introduced over drunken fish before we were scattered to opposite coasts of the Empire—there's a Chinese poem to be written there), Nicholas Jenkins, who gave them the thumbs-up.

M. H.

INTRODUCTION

In 1946 or 1947, at a late-ish midpoint of his life, but effectively when his career was beginning (all three, mid-point, career, and life were rather skewed by the Third Reich), Günter Eich prepared a CV to be made public at a reading or readings. He had recently written poems ("Camp 16" and "Inventory" and others) that were a departure from his early manner and wanted to indicate as much, and perhaps to warn listeners. I quote the whole of it, partly for the facts, partly for the dry pleasure of Eich's understatement:

> I was born on 1 February 1907 in Lebus, a little one-horse town that now straddles the German border. From the hills on the left bank of the Oder I can look across the river and see the house I was born in, now in Polish hands. I grew up in various towns and villages dotted over Brandenburg. My earliest aim in life was to be a coachman. But once I learned to read, this rather exact ambition was somehow smudged by Meyer's encyclopedia, the weightiest book in my father's possession. The world was full of color and complication, that was what I took from this miracle of erudition. Unfortunately, we didn't have the volumes from *R* to *Z*—and the want of them shows in me to this day.

> When we moved to Berlin just before the end of World War I, I attended a theater for the first time in my life. I went home and started writing plays in iambic pentameter. And so my school years came and went, until in spite of my total ignorance of the steam engine, I managed to pass my exams. In accordance with my father's wishes, I studied law and jurisprudence, and on the side, from my own unfathomable inclinations, Oriental languages. A year spent in Paris fed my inclination toward the arts and weakened any aspirations to bourgeois solidity. From 1932, I lived as a freelance writer, in Dres-

den, Berlin, and finally in a village on the Pomeranian coast. In August 1939 I was drafted into the Wehrmacht for a six-week training course. A little late, in summer 1945, I came back, restored to the status of civilian, but with the balance of my goods and chattels on the far side of the Oder-Neisse-Line. I am presently living in Bavaria, as a registered refugee with a backpack, in readiness for the next trek.

I wrote my first poems at the age of ten, and first saw my name in print at twenty. The poems I have for you now came about after ten years in which I didn't write a line, in POW camp and after. They do not mean to project the reader or listener into a more beautiful world; their aim is to be objective.[1]

This was the second "moment," so to speak, in Eich's poetry: the moment of the Zero Hour and *Germania rasa*, the moment of plain speech after the hateful jargon and lying bluster of Nazism, the moment of the frank avowal and litany of destitution. And it is at this moment that this book begins.

Eich's actual beginnings—the sentimental, derivative, and conventionally lyrical poems in *Gedichte* (1930) and after—promised nothing beyond a minor career in provincial letters. He was scathing later about his early work and, Betjeman-like, had cause to be grateful to the Allied bomb that in 1943 demolished his flat in Berlin, taking his manuscripts with it. When he reappeared as a poet, "after ten years in which I didn't write a line," he was unrecognizable. I wouldn't even say it was influence, but Eich's poems, humble and lived-in and somehow practical, deserve to be set alongside the Classical Chinese poems he studied and later translated, by and about priests and hermits and wanderers—the sort of thing of which Seamus Heaney wrote, "enviable stuff—/ Unfussy and believable"—with their minimal assertions of flat circumstances, the mischief that can be done by a new calendar or a smell of baking, the loneliness of life in a hole in the ground, without one's dead companions. When Eich first read from them at an early meeting of the Gruppe 47 in 1950, his peers, hearing him, sensed right away that they were dealing with writing of a superior order and awarded him their inaugural prize. (They had managed to raise a sponsor from somewhere; later they—Böll, Grass, etcetera—stumped up for it themselves.)

1. Translated from Günter Eich, *Werke* (Frankfurt: Suhrkamp Verlag, 1991), 4: 464.

And it was perfect, because, on reflection, Eich did exactly what the Gruppe 47 was called into being to do: to cleanse and adjust and simplify the language. ("Inventory"—"Inventur"—remains one of the most widely read poems in German, of any date; it makes a haunting pair with its exact contemporary, Paul Celan's "Todesfuge.")

But that is only beginning. Eich, to his great credit, continued to develop. His second moment, so to speak, is the unease within his own skin that he experienced and gave voice to in the fifties and sixties, as wounds healed, and civilization, so to speak, grew back. Eich was a political poet in a generation that was only just learning to be political again. His admirers were often half a generation or a generation younger than himself, and they didn't have his instinctive purity of style and outlook. While what they wrote was manifestly political, it was often not a poem, or not literature; it was they who were to decree, a little later, that novels were bourgeois or poems impossible. Their first love was politics, their second everything else; and Eich was always a poet. They were always embattled; he, seemingly, never—though of course even naming his sequence of tiny pieces "Long Poems" contains some sort of witty or implied rebuke. Eich wrote on Germany at the time of the Economic Miracle, the *Wirtschaftswunder*, the decade that Gunter Grass—a later 47er—called "die falschen Fünfziger," the fake fifties. Where for Rilke, thirty, forty, fifty years earlier, the poet's imperative had been to praise, for Eich it was to unsettle, disturb, provoke, rile. "Seid Sand im Getriebe," gum up the works, was his very widely circulated injunction. The unsleeping or rebellious conscience of the individual was the only possible weapon against a normative, dulling, and complacent society—and always, by implication, a return of totalitarianism. In his poems and radio plays—a genre in which he was both a pioneer and an acknowledged master—and in the poems *in* his radio plays, like those included here from his best-known piece, "Dreams" (1951), Eich warns. He is a German sibyl, as compressed and oblique as the Greek original. In him, wisdom becomes picture.

Eich wrote relatively little, and most of what he wrote was short. He had no sideline in theoretical or critical prose, wrote no fiction or autobiography, only the poems and radio plays, and in the 1960s, perhaps fearing any sort of regular or predictable production, he seemed to set even those aside, and turned instead to puppet plays—a pyrrhic form, if ever there was one—and a personally evolved genre he called "*Maulwürfe*" ("moles"), something seditiously uncategorizable between a prose poem and a Kafka short story. His personal life was as quietly surprising: he lived with the writer Ilse Aichinger (whom he married in 1953) in various villages in Bavaria and Austria—one lovely address was Kirchstrasse 71¼ —a quiet rusticity punctuated with long and exotic, and for the period, unusually wide-ranging reading tours that took him all over the world, mostly on behalf of the Goethe Institute. In 1955 he was in Portugal; in 1960, Yugoslavia; in 1961, the Balkans and the Near East; in 1962, Asia; in 1963, Scandinavia; in 1966, West Africa; in 1967, Iran, and so on. These travels—which make themselves felt in a strained or diluted way in the poems—are perhaps the only external mark of success in Eich's life. Because Eich seems to have been entirely without the careerist ambitions of most poets—even the successful ones. Books were tickled out of him by impatient or silver-tongued publishers; prizes came to him without anxiety or agitation on his part: the most important radio drama prize, the Hörspielpreis der Kriegsblinden (Radio Play Award from the War-Blind) in 1953; the most important German literary prize, the Georg Büchner Preis, in 1959. In few, rather obscure and determinedly downbeat interviews he made no bones about his moods or perspectives:

> *Good morning, Herr Eich, welcome!*
>
> Good morning, Herr Thoma.
>
> *Herr Eich, the principal field of your literary endeavors is the radio play, is that correct?*
>
> Yes, well, it used to be.
>
> *Used to be? You mean to say it no longer is?*
>
> Oh Lord, I didn't mean it to come out like that. I expect I'll write another radio play some time, but at the moment the prospect seems a little remote.[2]

It is entitled, with ringing implausibility, "What Really Interests Me Is Language." The whole thing—an interview from 1967—is like being politely turned away at the door by a nicely turned out, but still grumpy, old man.

2. Ibid., p. 504.

Eich won't have been the first or last poet to refuse to play ball; to protect the sources of his creativity, while at the same time being utterly, even alarmingly, frank about his morale and personal circumstances. (He reminds me a little of the way I used to reply to "How are you?" in English, before I understood it wasn't a question.) No reader of the poems will be surprised by Eich's *nolo*. After all, here is the man, or the voice, that declares what little use he has for the spa, or for Mexico, or society weddings. "I prefer/ to lay lettuce leaves / in a sandwich," he says, "and stay in the wrong." Most characteristically he is looking back on things, or at the end of things; summer is over, August is over, the thriller is finished (what will he do without it?), the biography has been set down, it is "too late for modesty," papers are "posthumous." Often too the poet is sitting on packed bags, waiting to move off into the new era; "greetings, cemeteries!" he declares boisterously, or he makes plans—hardly likely—to see in the new millennium, or to feast in the grave at the price of an obol. Things don't transpire as he would wish, or again he is uneasy in some strangely altered reality, as when he is driven out of his home—by herrings, wouldn't you know it. It isn't that tedious getout, surrealism, by the way; it's merely what poetry is supposed to do: "thinking in images." To my mind, there's something in Eich of Paul Klee's pictures: both are home-made, modest in scale, immediately delightful, inventive, cogent. An Eich poem too can be a space shared with fish, or color, or a large arrow. Both Eich and Klee have a childlike quality, while not being in the least childish: an adult precociousness. Günter Eich, as much as Anton Webern (her subject at the beginning) or Klee or any of the others listed, has the kind of pioneering modern qualities that Elizabeth Bishop once tentatively identified:

> I am crazy about some of the short instrumental pieces. They seem exactly like what I'd always wanted, vaguely, to hear and never had, and really "contemporary." That strange kind of modesty that I think one feels in almost everything contemporary one really likes—Kafka, say, or Marianne [Moore], or even Eliot, and Klee and Kokoschka and Schwitters . . . Modesty, care, *space*, a sort of helplessness but determination at the same time.[3]

3. *Words in Air: The Complete Correspondence between Elizabeth Bishop and Robert Lowell*, ed. Thomas Travisano and Saskia Hamilton (New York: Farrar, Straus and Giroux, 2008), p. 250.

Eich is a great poet of temperament. Even English, with its famously extensive vocabulary, has trouble, I think, finding words for him—I think fortuitously of the closing lines of this selection, "The gray of parrot feathers / eludes description"—and that's without even thinking of America, with its reflex shudder at anything "negative" or "pessimistic," much less "morbid." I would argue that there is a kind of temperament trap around Eich. One may use words like bitter, sour, grouchy, grumpy, gloomy, mordant, tart, but none of them gets the speed or the adroitness or the surprisingness or the sheer pleasure of these poems. There is nothing muddy or lingering or predictable about the writing, which is urgent, clear, and warm. The poems are not—one might think of someone like Larkin—self-steeped; each one, even the smallest of them, say, "Roman Footnote" or "Perspective from the *Spezial-Keller*" or "Old Postcards, 11" is a brisk and honest negotiation with the world. Yes, the gestures of many of them—beginning with their brief dimensions and clipped speech—are of refusal, but that doesn't make them negative. Rather, Eich affirms one of the most ancient human freedoms, that of saying "no." He is irascible, pessimistic, solitary, misanthropic, but these are all sources of joy, for him and for the reader. A German critic has said that "late Eich"—and my selection is mainly "late", everything is from the second half of Eich's life, and a lot of it from his last five years—might one day come to have a significance and weight similar to "late Beethoven." In form, content, personnel, and psychological equipment, these poems are reduced to their barest minimum. Indeed, in some of the best and most moving of them—"Two in the Afternoon," "Half," "Confined to Bed," "Optics," "Names," "Hospital Colors"—consciousness is further disciplined and bent by sensory impairment or illness. In the hour of its death, a blind dog dreams and mistakes; human deafness, forgetfulness, fears (those "enemies" that make their appearance in a surprising number of the poems), dimming sight, and isolation condition a sharper, stranger world through which the poem must make its way. In the end, it seems to me, in a piece like "And," Eich was making poems almost without words.

I don't think there's much to say about my translations, but then I probably always think that. It's a matter of coming to Eich's conclusions with getting on for as much grace, surprise, celerity, and quiddity as he displays in his originals. I haven't taken any very great liberties—I might say I haven't had to. As I generally do, I've always had in mind the reader with nothing but English. I've therefore used my own poetic instincts and intelligence—

well, it seemed better than not using them. On occasion, I've reversed the order of phrases, more rarely of whole sentences. I've sometimes written a more leisurely English, thinking that (for reason of its fabled understatement) it would work better, as in "I don't think I can stay here." I've occasionally sharpened elements in the German, as in "*nosing* down the hill," and even gone so far as adding the odd word, the bakers, for instance, "stretching in the *pale* morning wind." I've put "bagpipes" for "blowpipe," and "rhinoceros" where the German would seem to require "hippopotamus"; it's done for the associations of stubbornness and cruelty in its thick skin; "hippopotamus" is too frivolous a word in English be in any way helpful. Poems from radio plays—I have done the celebrated poems from *Träume* (Dreams) of 1951—and the sonorous "Rain in Eltville" and the terrifying "Examine Your Fingertips" are in a different category again: not pared down, but bouncy, public, and rhetorical. They have been translated accordingly, specifically the poem "Dreams," with concrete detail to match from various parts of the English-speaking world. My thinking is that we are so much more mongrel and global than we were then, and I haven't wanted to leave the poem as a sort of period piece.

I think I've evolved in these translations a specific diction to treat with Eich: *mulish, crimped, pashminas, safety matches, squabble, humans, looped, grandstand, tippling, proposed itself.* Not exactly showy or difficult, much less obscure words, but words that have a quality of relict or disject, a certain melancholy residue of boisterousness, that imply perhaps a more systematic and thoroughgoing vocabulary and a more powerful grammatical current to wash them ashore, words that have a quality of having been beached. Here, I realize, is for me a source of the quiet and immense and eerie power of Eich: words are like stray, chance, isolated survivals after some catastrophe, of unpredictable utility and beauty, most likely misapplied and unhelpful in any given context, like the "sodden ruches" of a waitress's blouse. Eich was, after all, a great admirer and appreciator of Beckett's. If there is any licence I have taken, it may have been that.

Michael Hofmann
March 2009

from _Abgelegene Gehöfte_

Remote Smallholdings (1948)

ABGELEGENE GEHÖFTE

Die Hühner und Enten treten
den Hof zu grünlichem Schmutz.
Die Bauern im Hause beten.
Von den Mauern bröckelt der Putz.

Der Talgrund zeichnet Mäander
in seine Wiesen hinein.
Die Weide birgt Alexander,
Cäsarn der Brennesselstein.

Auch wo die Spinnen weben,
der Spitz die Bettler verbellt,
im Rübenland blieben am Leben
die großen Namen der Welt.

Die Ratten pfeifen im Keller,
ein Vers schwebt im Schmetterlingslicht,
die Säfte der Welt treiben schneller,
Rauch steigt wie ein feurig Gedicht.

REMOTE SMALLHOLDINGS

The ducks and hens
tread the farmyard to a shitty green.
The smallholders are indoors praying.
Plaster crumbles off the walls.

The little stream meanders
through its soggy meadow.
The willow harbors Alexander,
Caesar is in the nettle stone.

The great names of the world
are at large in the beet-fields,
for all that spiders weave,
and the spitz barks at vagrants.

Rats pipe in the cellar,
a line of verse skims in the butterfly light,
the saps of the world learn to circulate,
smoke rises like a fiery poem.

PFANNKUCHENREZEPT

Die Trockenmilch der Firma Harrison Brothers, Chikago,
das Eipulver von Walkers, Merrymaker & Co, Kingstown, Alabama,
das von der deutschen Campführung nicht unterschlagene Mehl
und die Zuckerration von drei Tagen
ergeben, gemischt mit dem gut gechlorten Wasser des Altvaters
    Rhein,
einen schönen Pfannkuchenteig.
Man brate ihn in der Schmalzportion für acht Mann
auf dem Deckel einer Konservenbüchse und über dem Feuer
von lange gedörrtem Gras.
Wenn ihr ihn dann gemeinsam verzehrt,
jeder sein Achtel,
oh dann spürt ihr, wenn er auf der Zunge zergeht,
in einer üppigen Sekunde das Glück der geborgenen Kindheit,
wo ihr in die Küche euch schlichet, ein Stück
Teig zu erbetteln in der Vorweihnachtszeit,
oder ein Stück Waffel, weil Besuch gekommen war am
    Sonntagnachmittag,
spürt ihr in der schnell vergangenen Sekunde allen
Kuchenduft der Kinderjahre, habt noch einmal
fest gepackt den Schürzenzipfel der Mutter,
oh Ofenwärme, Mutterwärme, – bis ihr
wieder erwacht und die Hände leer sind
und ihr euch hungrig anseht und wieder
mürrisch zurückgeht ins Erdloch. Der Kuchen
war auch nicht richtig geteilt gewesen und immer
muß man aufpassen, daß man nicht zu kurz kommt.

RECIPE FOR PANCAKES

Powdered milk from the firm of Harrison Bros., Chicago,
dried egg from Walker's, Merrymaker & Co., of Kingstown,
    Alabama,
any flour left unconfiscated by the German camp direction,
and three days' ration of sugar,
when stirred with properly chlorinated water from Father Rhine,
make an excellent pancake batter.
Fry it on a tin lid
in the lard portion for eight men
over a fire of withered grass.
When you then come to eat it,
each man his eighth,
as it melts in the mouth, you will,
for one scrumptious second, sample the delight of a pampered
    childhood,
where you snuck into the kitchen to beg for
a spoonful of raw cake mix from the bowl in the time before
    Christmas,
or a piece of waffle because it was Sunday afternoon and there were
    visitors,
in that fleeting second you will sniff all
the kitchen aromas of childhood, you will have caught
hold of your mother's apron,
oh stove warmth, mother warmth—till you
come round, and you see that your hands are empty
and you look at one another hungrily and slouch back
to your hole in the ground. Nor are the portions
all alike either, and you have to see to it
that you get your rightful share.

CAMP 16

Durch den Stacheldraht schau ich
grad auf das Fließen des Rheins.
Ein Erdloch daneben bau ich,
ein Zelt hab ich keins.

Ich habe auch keine Decke.
Der Mantel blieb in Opladen.
Wenn ich ins Erdloch mich strecke,
find ich keinen Kameraden.

Zur Lagerstatt rupf ich Luzerne.
Nachts sprech ich mit mir allein.
Zu Häupten mir funkeln die Sterne,
es flüstert verworren der Rhein.

Bald wird die Luzerne verdorrt sein,
der Himmel sich finster bezieht,
im Fließen des Rheins wird kein Wort sein,
das mir süß einschläfert das Lid.

Nichts wird sein als der Regen, –
mich schützt kein Dach und kein Damm, –
zertreten wird auf den Wegen
das Grün des Frühlings zu Schlamm.

Wo blieben die Kameraden?
Ach, bei Regen und Sturm
wollen zu mir sich laden
nur Laus und Regenwurm.

CAMP 16

I look through the barbed wire
directly at the flowing Rhine.
I dig myself a hole in the ground,
I have no tent.

I have no blanket either.
My coat is still in Opladen.
When I stretch out in my hole,
I don't encounter any comrade.

For my bed I pluck lucerne.
At night I talk to myself.
The stars glitter overhead,
the Rhine murmurs to me.

Soon the lucerne will be dry,
the sky will cloud over,
the flowing of the Rhine will be without
words to send me off to sleep.

There will be nothing but rain—
no roof and no wall protects me—
on the paths the green
of spring will be trodden to slime.

Where are my comrades?
Oh, when it rains and storms,
the only ones to seek my company
are the louse and the earthworm.

INVENTUR

Dies ist meine Mütze,
dies ist mein Mantel,
hier mein Rasierzeug
im Beutel aus Leinen.

Konservenbüchse:
Mein Teller, mein Becher,
ich hab in das Weißblech
den Namen geritzt.

Geritzt hier mit diesem
kostbaren Nagel,
den vor begehrlichen
Augen ich berge.

Im Brotbeutel sind
ein Paar wollene Socken
und einiges, was ich
niemand verrate,

so dient es als Kissen
nachts meinem Kopf.
Die Pappe hier liegt
zwischen mir und der Erde.

Die Bleistiftmine
lieb ich am meisten:
Tags schreibt sie mir Verse,
die nachts ich erdacht.

INVENTORY

This is my cap,
my coat,
my shaving kit
in the burlap bag.

This tin can:
my plate and my cup,
I scratched my name
in the soft metal.

Scratched it with this
precious nail,
which I keep out of sight
of thieving eyes.

In my bread bag is
a pair of woollen socks
and some other things
I don't tell anyone about,

it serves me as a pillow
for my head at night.
This piece of card I lay
between my body and the ground.

The pencil lead
is my favorite:
by day it writes out lines
that come to me at night.

Dies ist mein Notizbuch,
dies meine Zeltbahn,
dies ist mein Handtuch,
dies ist mein Zwirn.

This is my notebook,
this my canvas,
my towel,
my thread.

ERSTER JANUAR

Nur ein Kalender spricht morgens vom neuen Jahre,
die Wände wissen, daß nichts Neues beginnt.
Draußen die Wolken flattern wie immer so leicht wie Haare,
und an die Fenster greift mit denselben Händen der Wind.

März und April wird kommen, und später
füllt dich ein Tag mit ewigen Stunden aus,
fällt mit Himmel und mit geblähter
Wolke in deine Hände und in dein Haus.

Manchmal erblickst du dich nachts in einem Spiegel,
das Gesicht undeutlich von Altern erfüllt,
wie ein verblichener Brief mit nie geöffnetem Siegel,
der immer die gleiche Schrift verhüllt.

Alle Tage sind neu und sind Jubiläen,
aber der Schmerz ist fern,
und du hast von den ewigen Trophäen
nur noch den Abendstern.

FIRST OF JANUARY

Only a calendar would start the day by talking about a new year,
the walls know damn well this isn't the start of anything new.
Outside, as ever, the clouds blow past, light as hair,
and the wind rattles the windows with the same hands.

March and April will come, and eventually
a day will fill you with its endless hours;
along with the sky and the blown clouds
it will fall into your hands and your house.

Sometimes you catch your face at night in a mirror
obscurely filled with aging—
a faded envelope with unbroken seal,
stuffed always with the same script.

Every day is new and a jubilee,
but pain is a long way off,
and of the celestial trophies
the only one in your possession is the evening star.

from *Botschaften des Regens*

Messages from the Rain (1955)

ENDE EINES SOMMERS

Wer möchte leben ohne den Trost der Bäume!

Wie gut, daß sie am Sterben teilhaben!
Die Pfirsiche sind geerntet, die Pflaumen färben sich,
während unter dem Brückenbogen die Zeit rauscht.

Dem Vogelzug vertraue ich meine Verzweiflung an.
Er mißt seinen Teil von Ewigkeit gelassen ab.
Seine Strecken
werden sichtbar im Blattwerk als dunkler Zwang,
die Bewegung der Flügel färbt die Früchte.

Es heißt Geduld haben.
Bald wird die Vogelschrift entsiegelt,
unter der Zunge ist der Pfennig zu schmecken.

END OF SUMMER

Who would want to live without the comfort of trees!

Aren't we lucky that they are mortal!
The peaches have been picked, the plums are coloring up
while time swoops under the bridge.

I confide my despair to the bird formations heading south.
Calmly they measure out their portion of eternity.
Their routes
become visible as a dark compulsion in the foliage.
The moving of wings colors the fruit.

We must be patient.
Soon the sky-writing of birds will be deciphered.
Don't you taste the copper penny under your tongue?

GEGENWART

An verschiedenen Tagen gesehen,
die Pappeln der Leopoldstraße,
aber immer herbstlich,
immer Gespinste nebliger Sonne
oder von Regengewebe.

Wo bist du, wenn du neben mir gehst?
Immer Gespinste aus entrückten Zeiten,
zuvor und zukünftig:
Das Wohnen in Höhlen,
die ewige troglodytische Zeit,
der bittere Geschmack vor den Säulen Heliogabals
und den Hotels von St. Moritz.
Die grauen Höhlen, Baracken,
wo das Glück beginnt,
dieses graue Glück.

Der Druck deines Armes, der mir antwortet,
der Archipelag, die Inselkette, zuletzt Sandbänke,
nur noch erahnbare Reste
aus der Süße der Vereinigung.

(Aber du bist von meinem Blute,
über diesen Steinen, neben den Gartensträuchern,
ausruhenden alten Männern auf der Anlagenbank
und dem Rauschen der Straßenbahnlinie sechs,
Anemone, gegenwärtig

THE PRESENT

Glimpsed on various days,
the poplars on Leopoldstrasse,
but always autumnal,
always wraiths of misty sunshine
or bits of rain-embroidery.

Where are you, when you walk at my side?
Always wraiths from distant times,
past and to come:
dwelling in caves,
the endless troglodytic period,
the bitter taste of the columns of Heliogabalus
and the hotels of St. Moritz.
The gray caves, tenements
where happiness begins,
gray happiness.

The pressure of your arm answering me,
the archipelago, the chain of islands, latterly sandbanks,
dimly perceived residue
of the sweetness of our conjunction.

(But you are of my blood,
over these stones, beside the garden shrubs,
old men resting on the park bench
and the rumbling of the number 6 tram,
anemone, present

mit der Macht des Wassers im Aug
und der Feuchtigkeit der Lippe –)

Und immer Gespinste, die uns einspinnen,
Aufhebung der Gegenwart,
ungültige Liebe,
der Beweis, daß wir zufällig sind,
geringes Laub an Pappelbäumen
und einberechnet von der Stadtverwaltung,
Herbst in den Rinnsteinen
und die beantworteten Fragen des Glücks.

with the power of water in your eye
and the freshness of your lip.)

And always wraiths, spinning us in,
suspension of the present,
unvalid love,
proof that we are subject to chance,
sparse poplar leaves
factored in by the municipality,
autumn in the gutters,
the questions posed by happiness satisfactorily answered.

D-ZUG MÜNCHEN-FRANKFURT

Die Donaubrücke von Ingolstadt,
Das Altmühltal, Schiefer bei Solnhofen,
in Treuchtlingen Anschlußzüge –
Dazwischen
Wälder, worin der Herbst verbrannt wird,
Landstraßen in den Schmerz,
Gewölk, das an Gespräche erinnert,
flüchtige Dörfer, von meinem Wunsch erbaut,
in der Nähe deiner Stimme zu altern.

Zwischen den Ziffern der Abfahrtszeiten
breiten sich die Besitztümer unserer Liebe aus.
Ungetrennt
bleiben darin die Orte der Welt,
nicht vermessen und unauffindbar.

Der Zug aber
treibt an Gunzenhausen und Ansbach
und an Mondlandschaften der Erinnerung
– der sommerlich gewesene Gesang
der Frösche von Ornbau –
vorbei.

MUNICH-FRANKFURT EXPRESS

Bridge over the Danube at Ingolstadt,
the Altmühl valley, slates at Solnhofen,
connections at Treuchtlingen—
and in between
forests in which autumn is a bonfire,
roads going out into pain,
clouds reminiscent of conversations,
flashing by villages built of my desire
to grow old in the vicinity of your voice.

Between departure times
the properties of our love are spread out.
There
the places of the world remain undivided,
not surveyed, and not findable.

The train, however,
barrels through Gunzenhausen and Ansbach,
the lunar landscapes of memory
—the summery song
of the frogs of Ornbau—
all in our wake.

KLEINE REPARATUR

Kleine Reparatur: Flammenstoß aus Karbid.
Es genügt ein Mann.
Ein Riß, sagt er, im Geländer der Brücke.

Eine Heftpflaster-Wunde.
So sagt er, um uns zu täuschen,
denn Krankheiten gehen um im Drahtsystem der Erde.
Telefonleitungen und Erdkabel verbreiten sie weiter,
Lues, Tuberkulose, Krebs, Leukämie,
Krankheiten, die dem Metall nicht zukommen.
Man hat sie zu spät erkannt.

Aber was hätte man aufhalten können?
Vielleicht liegt dem eine Absicht zugrunde:
Es könnte sein, daß eine Rangänderung im Gange ist.
Das erste, was der Mensch abgeben muß,
sind seine Krankheiten.
Später das andere.

MINOR REPAIR

Minor repair: carbide flame.
A single workman is enough.
A crack in the bridge rail, he says.

A sticking-plaster job,
he says, to throw us off the scent,
because illnesses are doing the rounds in the world's wiring.
Phone lines and cables pass them on:
syphilis, tuberculosis, cancer, leukemia—
illnesses one wouldn't have expected in metal.
They were diagnosed too late.

But how could we have prevented them?
Perhaps there is some purpose in it.
It might be that the whole of existence is being reordered.
They begin by taking from us
our diseases.
Everything else by and by.

WEG ZUM BAHNHOF

Noch schweigt die Fabrik,
verödet im Mondschein.
Das Frösteln des Morgens
wollt ich gewohnt sein!

Rechts in der Jacke
die Kaffeeflasche,
die frierende Hand
in der Hosentasche,

so ging ich halb schlafend
zum Sechsuhrzug,
mich griffe kein Trauern,
ich wär mir genug.

Nun aber rührt der warme Hauch
aus den Bäckerein
mein Herz an wie eine Zärtlichkeit
und ich kann nicht gelassen sein.

WAY TO THE STATION

The factory is still silent,
bleak in the moonlight.
I thought I was used to
the shiver of early morning!

With my thermos of coffee
in my jacket,
my freezing hand
in my trouser pocket,

I wandered half-asleep
to the six a.m. train,
thinking I was self-sufficient,
proof against all sadness.

But now the warm aroma
from the bakeries
touches my heart like a caress,
and makes it impossible to be calm.

LEMBERG

1

Stadt auf wievielen Hügeln.
Ergrautes Gelb.
Einen Glockenton gibt es dir mit,
hörbar im Klirren
deiner Erkennungsmarke.

2

Abhänge wie die Angst unzählbar.
Die Straßenbahn endet
in einer Steppe von Unkraut
vor abgegriffenen Türen.

LVOV

1

City on however many hills.
A grizzled yellow.
It gives you a memory of bells to take with you,
audible in the jingle
of your dog tag.

2

Slopes, like fears, too many to count.
The tramline ends
in front of peeling doors
in a prairie of weeds.

ANDENKEN

Die Moore, in die wir gehen wollten, sind trockengelegt.
Der Torf hat unsere Abende gewärmt.
Schwarzen Staub hebt der Wind auf.
Er bläst die Namen von den Grabsteinen
und trägt uns ein
mit diesem Tage.

MEMORIAL

The moors we wanted to hike have been drained.
Their turf has warmed our evenings.
The wind is full of black dust.
It scours the names off the gravestones
and etches this day
into us.

WO ICH WOHNE

Als ich das Fenster öffnete,
schwammen Fische ins Zimmer,
Heringe. Es schien
eben ein Schwarm vorüberzuziehen.
Auch zwischen den Birnbäumen spielten sie.
Die meisten aber
hielten sich noch im Wald,
über den Schonungen und den Kiesgruben.

Sie sind lästig. Lästiger aber sind noch
die Matrosen
(auch höhere Ränge, Steuerleute, Kapitäne),
die vielfach ans offene Fenster kommen
und um Feuer bitten für ihren schlechten Tabak.

Ich will ausziehen.

WHERE I LIVE

When I opened the window
fishes swam into the room,
herrings. A school of them
must just have been passing.
I saw some playing among the pear trees as well.
There were more of them
in the woods,
over the conifer plantations and gravel pits.

They are a nuisance. But even more annoying
are the sailors
(some high-ranking ones among them too, helmsmen, captains),
who keep coming up to the open window
and asking for a light for their beastly tobacco.

I don't think I can stay here.

REISE

Du kannst dich abwenden
vor der Klapper des Aussätzigen,
Fenster und Ohren verschließen
und warten, bis er vorbei ist.

Doch wenn du sie einmal gehört hast,
hörst du sie immer,
und weil er nicht weggeht,
mußt du gehen.

Packe ein Bündel zusammen, das nicht zu schwer ist,
Denn niemand hilft tragen.
Mach dich verstohlen davon und laß die Tür offen,
du kommst nicht wieder.

Geh weit genug, ihm zu entgehen,
fahre zu Schiff oder suche die Wildnis auf:
Die Klapper des Aussätzigen verstummt nicht.

Du nimmst sie mit, wenn er zurückbleibt.
Horch, wie das Trommelfell klopft
vom eigenen Herzschlag!

JOURNEY

You can turn away
from the leper's rattle,
close your ears and windows
and wait for him to go.

But when you've heard it once,
you will always hear it,
and because he won't leave,
you will have to.

Pack a bundle, not too heavy,
because no one will help you carry it.
Sneak out, and leave the door open behind you,
you'll not be back.

Travel far to get clear of him,
take ship or go out into the wilderness:
the rattle of the leper will never stop.

You'll take it with you while he stays behind.
That boom-boom-boom in your ears—
it's the sound of your own heart!

MITTAGS UM ZWEI

Der graue Spitz des Pfarrers
an der Sakristeitür.
Vor seinen erblindenden Augen
schwirren im Sand die Flügel der Sperlinge.

Er spürt wie Erinnerungen
die Schnur des Fasanenbündels,
die in der Friedhofsmauer als Riß erschien,
das Beben der Grabsteine,
wenn die Raupe buckelt vorm lähmenden Stich,
die Verfärbung der Ziegel
beim Schrei des sterbenden Maulwurfs.

Gelassen vernimmt er
das Gerücht aus den Wäldern,
die Tore des Paradieses würden geöffnet.

TWO IN THE AFTERNOON

The minister's gray spitz
at the sacristy door.
Sparrows' wings scuffle in the dirt
in front of his sightless eyes.

Like memories to him:
the twine tying the brace of pheasants
that appeared as a crack in the cemetery wall;
the shaking of the gravestones
when the crippled caterpillar wriggles;
the discoloration of the bricks
in the scream of the dying mole.

Calmly he acknowledges
the report from the woods
that the gates of paradise are to be thrown open.

BETRACHTET DIE FINGERSPITZEN

Betrachtet die Fingerspitzen, ob sie sich schon verfärben!

Eines Tages kommt sie wieder, die ausgerottete Pest.
Der Postbote wirft sie als Brief in den rasselnden Kasten,
als eine Zuteilung von Heringen liegt sie dir im Teller,
die Mutter reicht sie dem Kinde als Brust.

Was tun wir, da niemand mehr lebt von denen,
die mit ihr umzugehen wußten?
Wer mit dem Entsetzlichen gut Freund ist,
kann seinen Besuch in Ruhe erwarten.
Wir richten uns immer wieder auf das Glück ein,
aber es sitzt nicht gern auf unseren Sesseln.

Betrachtet die Fingerspitzen! Wenn sie sich schwarz färben,
ist es zu spät.

EXAMINE YOUR FINGERTIPS

Examine your fingertips for signs of discoloration!

One day it will be back, the supposedly eradicated contagion.
The postman will drop it in the rattling letterbox along with the
    circulars,
it will fetch up on your plate with a portion of herring,
the breastfeeding mother will give it to her babe.

What shall we do, as none of those who would habitually confront it
are still alive?
Whoever is on a reasonable footing with horror
can expect its coming with equanimity.
We are forever making space for happiness
but how often does it agree to sit on our chairs?

Examine your fingertips! If they are black,
it is already too late.

BRIEFSTELLE

Keins von den Büchern werde ich lesen.

Ich erinnere mich
an die strohumflochtenen Stämme,
an die ungebrannten Ziegel in den Regalen.
Der Schmerz bleibt und die Bilder gehen.

Mein Alter will ich in der grünen Dämmerung
des Weins verbringen,
ohne Gespräch. Die Zinnteller knistern.

Beug dich über den Tisch! Im Schatten
vergilbt die Karte von Portugal.

FROM A LETTER

I shan't read any of the books.

I recall
the tree-trunks swaddled in straw,
the unburned tiles on the shelves.
Pictures go and the pain remains.

I want to spend my late years
without speech, in the green half-light
of wine. Tin plates clink.

Lean forward! That's the wall map
of Portugal yellowing in the shade.

EINSICHT

Alle wissen,
daß Mexiko ein erfundenes Land ist.

Als ich das Küchenspind öffnete,
fand ich die Wahrheit
zugedeckt
in den beschrifteten Büchsen.

Die Reiskörner
ruhen sich aus von den Jahrhunderten.
Vorm Fenster
setzt der Wind seinen Weg fort.

UNDERSTANDING

Everyone knows
that there is no such place as Mexico.

When I opened the kitchen cupboard
I found the truth
obscured
by labels on tins.

The rice grains
are resting after the centuries.
Outside
the wind goes on on its way.

ENDE AUGUST

Mit weißen Bäuchen hängen die toten Fische
zwischen Entengrütze und Schilf.
Die Krähen haben Flügel, dem Tod zu entrinnen.
Manchmal weiß ich, daß Gott
am meisten sich sorgt um das Dasein der Schnecke.
Er baut ihr ein Haus. Uns aber liebt er nicht.

Eine weiße Staubfahne zieht am Abend der Omnibus,
wenn er die Fußballmannschaft heimfährt.
Der Mond glänzt im Weidengestrüpp,
vereint mit dem Abendstern.
Wie nahe bist du, Unsterblichkeit, im Fledermausflügel,
im Scheinwerfer-Augenpaar,
das den Hügel herab sich naht.

END OF AUGUST

The white bellies of dead fish
loom among duckweed and rushes.
Crows have wings to enable them to escape death.
There are times I know that God
is most concerned with the fate of snails.
He builds them houses. We are not His favorites.

At night, the bus taking the football team home
leaves a white trail of dust.
The moon shines in the willow herb,
in concert with the evening star.
How near you are, immortality—in the wings of bats,
in the pair of headlights
nosing down the hill.

from *Zu den Akten*

Ad Acta (1964)

ALTE POSTKARTEN

1

Hier wollte ich Straßenbahnen anlegen
und schaukeln
auf der Kette des Kriegerdenkmals.
Ein Zeichen für Taubstumme.
Eine Predigt für die Bäcker,
die sich räkeln im Morgenwind.

2

Der Ausblick, allmählich
verfärbt von Leim,
Deckblätter und Straße
zerschnitten
vom selben Messer.
Die Asphaltierung ist
geplant wie das Sterben.

3

Zwei deutliche Schriften, –
eine Fahrradwanderung
zu Burgruinen.
Uns aber gehts gut.
Wir spielen im schwarzen Sand.
Wir kauen Brot
für die Risse in den Tapeten.

OLD POSTCARDS

1

This is where I wanted to set up tramlines,
and swing on the chain
around the war memorial.
A warning to deaf-mutes.
A homily to bakers
stretching in the pale morning wind.

2

The scene gradually
darkened by distemper,
paper and street
incised
by the same knife.
Macadamization and death
plan ahead.

3

Two hieroglyphs—
a bicycle path
to the ruined castle.
But we're all right.
We're playing in the black sand.
We're masticating bread
to seal the cracks in the wallpaper.

4

Blasrohre am Sedantag,
drei null vier,
ein Rot in den Linden.
Morgen morgen morgen.

5

Halte dich fest
an den Seilen der Gerber,
bis die Engel kommen
mit Schirmmütze und Schultertuch,
nach dem Zeugnis der Steine,
dem vertrauenswürdigen
Abdruck in Rauch.

4

Bagpipes on the anniversary of Sedan,
three-oh-four,
the lindens bloodshot.
Morning morning morning.

5

Hold on
to the tanners' ropes
till the angels come
with peaked caps and pashminas,
to go by the evidence on the stones,
the reliable
impression of smoke.

NEUE POSTKARTEN

1

Triste Lastwagen und
Restaurants, an die ich nicht glaube.
O liebes Herbstlaub
und der Wind
durch slowenische Zimmer.

2

Sei bedankt, aber verlaß uns.
In den Höhlen der Rattenfänger
waren wir längst.

3

Oder, mein Fluß, erklärbar
aus Quellen und Nebenflüssen,
mein Morgengewinn, meine Unruh,
meine Sanduhr über den Ländern.

4

Mühlen vermisse ich hier.
Das Wasser träge,
der Wind stockt.
Zeit für Walzwerke,
vielleicht Lehmgruben

NEW POSTCARDS

1

Sad trucks and
improbable restaurants.
O autumn leaves that I love
and the wind
through Slovenian rooms.

2

Thanks, but leave us.
We have already been to the caves
of the rat catchers.

3

Oder, my river, explainable
in terms of sources and tributaries,
my morning profit, my mainspring,
my sand-clock over the provinces.

4

Mills are what I miss here.
The water is sluggish,
the wind comes and goes.
Time for rolling mills,
clay pits maybe

und Scheunenbrand,
Hüte für
Kossäten.

5

Surinam und die Raupen.
Erinnere dich, Merian
Maria Sibylla,
ich war das rechte
gebogene Nelkenblatt.

and barn burnings,
hats for
crofters.

    5

Surinam and caterpillars.
Remember, my Merian guide
Maria Sibylla,
I was the clove leaf,
the crimped one on the right.

BERICHT AUS EINEM KURORT

Ich habe das Wasser noch nicht getrunken,
halte auch nichts davon.
Aber der Bahnhofsumbau
läßt an Zukunft denken,
das macht mich störrisch.

Mein Blutbild und Koniferenozon,
das Mißtrauen der Badeärzte.
Natur
ist eine Form der Verneinung.
Die Gedichte in der Kurzeitung
sind besser.

REPORT FROM A SPA

I haven't tried the water yet,
that can wait.
But the redecorated station
implies future,
which makes me mulish.

Corpuscle count and forest ozone,
suspicion of the spa doctors.
Nature
is a form of negation.
Better to stick to
the ditties in the spa newsletter.

NACHHUT

Steh auf, steh auf!
Wir werden nicht angenommen,
die Botschaft kam mit dem Schatten der Sterne.

Es ist Zeit, zu gehen wie die andern.
Sie stellten ihre Straßen und leeren Häuser
unter den Schutz des Mondes. Er hat wenig Macht.

Unsere Worte werden von der Stille aufgezeichnet.
Die Kanaldeckel heben sich um einen Spalt.
Die Wegweiser haben sich gedreht.

Wenn wir uns erinnerten an die Wegmarken der Liebe,
ablesbar auf Wasserspiegeln und im Wehen des Schnees!
Komm, ehe wir blind sind!

REARGUARD

Get up! Get up!
We have been rejected,
the news came with the shadows of the stars.

It's time we left like everyone else.
They placed their streets and their deserted houses
under the protection of the moon. It has little power.

Our words are being recorded by silence.
The manhole covers lift up a crack.
The signposts have been turned round.

If only we remembered the traces of love,
legible on the surface of water and in the blowing of snow!
Hurry, before we go blind!

REST

Gebleicht die Minuten,
die mir für Träume bleiben,
ein Strychnin an der Theke bestellt,
deinen Augen gehorsam.
Ich kann gehen und komme wieder
in die Muster deiner Bluse,
wenn es längst dämmert
über den Schiffslichtern.
Komm! Die Rechnungen
sind geschrieben,
aus den Trompeten fährt Staub.

REMNANT

Bleached minutes
left me for my dreams.
Obedient to your eyes,
I ordered a strychnine at the bar.
I am free to leave and will return
in the pattern of your blouse
as day breaks
over the ships' lights.
Come! The bills
have been made out,
the trumpets are clearing their throats.

ALTE HOLLÄNDER

Zu oft die Hirse vergessen
und das lederne Wams.
Laß uns weitertanzen
unter Sprichwörtern,
die Hunde
durch die Kirchen führen
und Blätter brechen
über Bathseba.

OLD DUTCH MASTERS

Regularly forgot the millet
and the leather jerkin.
Let us go on dancing
under proverbs,
lead our dogs
down the aisle,
and part the leaves
over Bathsheba.

BRÜDER GRIMM

Brennesselbusch.
Die gebrannten Kinder
warten hinter den Kellerfenstern.
Die Eltern sind fortgegangen,
sagten, sie kämen bald.

Erst kam der Wolf,
der die Semmeln brachte,
die Hyäne borgte sich den Spaten aus,
der Skorpion das Fernsehprogramm.

Ohne Flammen
brennt draußen der Brennesselbusch.
Lange
bleiben die Eltern aus.

BROTHERS GRIMM

Nettlebush.
The burnt children
wait behind the cellar windows.
Their parents have gone out,
saying they will be back soon.

First came the wolf,
bringing rolls,
the hyena wanted to borrow a garden fork,
the scorpion came for the TV guide.

Without flames
the nettlebush burns outside.
Their parents
are gone a long time.

ZU SPÄT FÜR BESCHEIDENHEIT

Wir hatten das Haus bestellt
und die Fenster verhängt,
hatten Vorräte genug in den Kellern,
Kohlen und Öl,
und zwischen Hautfalten
den Tod in Ampullen verborgen.

Durch den Türspalt sehn wir die Welt:
Einen geköpften Hahn,
der über den Hof rennt.

Er hat unsere Hoffnungen zertreten.
Wir hängen die Bettücher auf die Balkone
und ergeben uns.

TOO LATE FOR MODESTY

We had tidied the house
and boarded up the windows,
had put by sufficient provisions in the cellars,
coal and oil,
and hidden death in phials
in snug folds of skin.

Through the crack in the door we can see the world:
a headless rooster
running across the yard.

He has trampled all our hopes.
We hang the sheets out on the balconies
and surrender.

BESTELLUNG

Fünf Gänge,
sag es den hölzernen Mädchen,
für den Pfennig unter der Zunge,
und die Teller gewärmt.

Ihr habt uns hingehalten
mit Fasanen und Stör,
Burgunder und Bouillabaisse.
Tragt endlich die Speise auf,
die es nicht gibt,
und entkorkt die Wunder!

Dann wollen wir gern
die Mäuler öffnen
und was wir schuldig sind
zahlen.

ORDER

Five courses—
tell it to those wooden girls—
for the penny under our tongue
and we want the plates warmed.

You've been leading us on
with pheasant and sturgeon,
burgundy and bouillabaisse.
Hurry up and serve the dishes
that don't exist,
and uncork the marvels!

Then we won't mind
opening our mouths
and paying
what we owe.

TRAGTASCHE

Läden für Süßwaren
und Spirituosen,
Magazine voll Essig,
Bahnübergänge
und Berberitzen,
die Verszeile aus Zermatt
mitgenommen ins Alter,
schlecht verpackt,
und bei jedem Einkauf
fallen Tage aus den Taschen,
und der neige d'antan
hängt im Sohlenprofil,
daß die Verkäufer flüstern
und ein Lehrling kichert
hinter dem Weißkrautfaß.

HOLDALL

Shops for confectionery
and spirits,
stores of vinegar,
railway crossings
and barberries,
the line of poetry from Zermatt
brought along for our dotage,
poorly packed,
and with every purchase
days fall out of our bags,
and *neige d'antan*
sticks to our soles
so that the salesgirls whisper,
and a trainee giggles
behind the barrel of sauerkraut.

OHNE UNTERSCHRIFT

Die Antworten: Raupen unter der Rinde
gefällter Pappeln,
Essigbäume am Beginn der Steigung,
verdunstetes Wasser im Honigglas.

Eine Weltordnung durch Schnittblumen
und die gefällige Linie der Waldränder.
Einige Geheimnisse
an Windrädern aufbewahrt,
genug für Klarheit und Überdruß –

Keine Fragen mehr, Einverständnis,
überlappt von Tod.

UNSIGNED

The answers: caterpillars under the bark
of felled poplars,
sumac trees at the foot of the slope,
water evaporated in honey jars.

A world order of cut flowers
and the pleasing line of forest edges.
A few secrets
put by on windmills,
enough for clarity and a slight queasiness—

no more questions now, assent,
shading into death.

JAQUES DEVANT, FÜR VIELE

Ich verrate
das Geheimnis des fleißigen Schülers.
Kein Schilf hat geflüstert,
das Dickicht hielt dicht,
an keiner Mauer
Kreide für seinen Namen vergeudet,
kein Hauch in ein Telefon.

Ich verrate,
was niemand wissen will:
Jaques Devant ist lange tot.
Er hat ein Grab nahe den Pyrenäen,
er war schuldlos.

Ich kenne die Umstände:
Die Weingärten und die Kirchenführung
und die Küster, wie sie wechselten.
Ich verrate
ein altes Schärpentuch,
den verdorrten
Vorwurf der Gräser.

JAQUES DEVANT, FOR THE MANY

I hereby betray
the secret of the hardworking student.
No reeds whispered,
all the rushes kept shtum,
on no wall
was chalk expended on his name
or breath into a telephone.

I betray
what no one wants to hear:
Jaques Devant has been dead a long time.
He has a grave near the Pyrenees,
he was without blame.

I know the circumstances:
the wine-gardens, the church commission,
the roster of sextons.
I call in evidence
an old poncho
and the withered
reproach of the grasses.

AUFGELASSENES ZOLLAMT

Ein durchschnittliches Gepäck:
Gedanken in Plastikhüllen,
kein Zinn, keine Pfauenfedern,
Einsamkeit, geplättet
im Wäschekoffer.

Hier ist der Ort,
wo wir bleiben.

Niemand zieht den Schlagbaum hoch.
Niemand kommt,
niemand verläßt uns.
In den blinden Fenstern
wartet der Abdruck des Zöllners.

OLD CUSTOMSHOUSE

Routine baggage:
thoughts in cellophane folders;
no peacock feathers, no pewter;
loneliness, nicely pressed
in a valise.

This
is where we will stay.

No one will raise the barrier.
No one will come;
no one will leave.
The customs official's prints wait
in the blind windows.

AUSSICHT VOM SPEZIAL-KELLER

Kulissen vor meiner Trunksucht
und Rauch in den Etüden für Julia,
keine Erbschaft,
die mich anziehend machte,
und meine Freunde
sind mir noch nicht begegnet.

PERSPECTIVE FROM THE *SPEZIAL-KELLER*

A backdrop for my bibulousness
and smoke towards Julia's sketches,
no fortune
to make me attractive to anyone,
and my friends
have yet to show.

ZUNAHME

Daß es Seegurken gibt,
macht mich verdrießlich,
die Frage vor allem:
Habe ich sie früher
nicht bemerkt,
oder sind sie wirklich
häufiger geworden,
inzwischen?

INCREASE

The existence of sea cucumbers
bothers me,
especially the question:
did I fail
to notice them before,
or have there
really gotten to be
more of them?

AUSKÜNFTE AUS DEM NACHLASS

Nach dem Kalkofen befragt:
Iltisse wohnen dort
und freundliche Mädchen.

In den Schutthaufen
Anfänge von grauem Star,
die Schöpfung
nah vor der Lesebrille.

Ich höre wenig:
Die Gänge im Motor,
Hilferufe, wenn niemand ruft.

Immer habe ich Brennesseln geliebt,
und jetzt erfahren,
daß sie nützlich sind.

TIPS FROM THE POSTHUMOUS PAPERS

Asked after the limekiln:
polecats live there
and kindly girls.

To the scrap heap
the onset of cataracts,
creation right up against
my reading glasses.

I don't hear much:
gear changes,
silence full of screams.

I have always loved nettles,
and only now learned
of their usefulness.

UNGÜLTIGE LANDKARTE

Das Muster
von Regen und Schonung,
die Knoten von Dorfweihern, –
ich habe sie eingefärbt,
wie es mir notwendig war.

Meine lieben Spinnen
haben darüber gewebt,
ein zweites Muster,
dem ich zustimmte,
als ich fortging.

FRAUDULENT MAP

The patterns
of rainfall and afforestation,
the veins of village streams—
I colored them in
as I saw fit.

My beloved spiders
wove a second pattern
on top,
which I approved
before leaving.

TOPOGRAPHIE EINER SCHÖNEREN WELT

Vergeblich die böse Hoffnung,
daß die Schreie der Gemarterten
die Zukunft leicht machen:

Gib acht, wessen Stimme vor Rührung bebt,
wem es das Herz bewegt,
wenn der Walzenwechsel verkürzt wird
auf achtundzwanzig Minuten.

Seid gegrüßt, Friedhöfe!

TOPOGRAPHY OF A BETTER WORLD

Vain the cruel hope
that the screams of the tortured
might pave the way for a brighter future:

observe whose voice trembles with emotion,
whose heart is stirred
when the rolls are changed
at twenty-eight minute intervals.

Greetings, cemeteries!

FUSSNOTE ZU ROM

Ich werfe keine Münzen in den Brunnen,
ich will nicht wiederkommen.

Zuviel Abendland,
verdächtig.

Zuviel Welt ausgespart.
Keine Möglichkeit
für Steingärten.

ROMAN FOOTNOTE

I shan't throw any coins in the fountain,
I don't want to come back.

Too Western—
suspicious.

Too much of the world excluded.
No chance
of rock gardens.

from *Anlässe und Steingärten*

Occasions and Rock Gardens (1966)

TIMETABLE

Diese Flugzeuge
zwischen Boston und Düsseldorf.
Entscheidungen aussprechen
ist Sache der Nilpferde.
Ich ziehe vor,
Salatblätter auf ein
Sandwich zu legen und
unrecht zu behalten.

TIMETABLE

These planes trafficking
between Boston and Düsseldorf.
To give a verdict
you have to be a rhinoceros.
I prefer
to lay lettuce leaves
in a sandwich
and stay in the wrong.

BERLIN 1918

Das meiste zwischen Zoo,
Potsdamer Bahnhof, Molkenmarkt,
der Kaiser und die spanische Grippe,
Ereignisse und Konfektion,
ein totes Gesicht in den Kissen, Oktober,
alles was über Wanzen zu wissen ist,
alles über den Kellner Albert, die tristen
Fahrten aufs Land, immer schon
die fehlenden Zusammenhänge,
die Kinderstunden vorm Ausguß,
alles Hauptwörter, die Grippe,
Otto der Schütz, der Kaiser, alles
zwischen Holzmarktstraße und
Landwehrkanal, November.

BERLIN, 1918

Mostly between Zoo,
Potsdam Station, Molkenmarkt,
the Kaiser and the Spanish 'flu,
events and tailoring,
a dead face on the pillows, October,
all there is to know about bedbugs,
all there is about Albert the waiter, the sad
trips out into the countryside, the missing
connections even then,
the childhood hours in front of the sink,
all the nouns, influenza,
Otto der Schütz, the Kaiser, everything
between Holzmarktstrasse and
Landwehrkanal, November.

KINDER- UND HAUSMÄRCHEN

Auf Rübenäckern zuhause,
Sternickel,
ein wilhelminischer Mörder,
steinern, wie wars
mit den Pfeffertüten,
den Verfolgern, die sich
die Augen rieben, überall
versagen die Quellen, ich möchte
meiner Heineschen Großmutter glauben,
sie erfand gut und kannte
die Hohlwege mit Teufelszwirn,
suchte die Taufpaten aus,
verwahrte auch
rohe Eier in der Kommode, ihr
danke ich manche Abneigungen,
zum Beispiel gegen
Sonnenauf-, Sonnenuntergänge,
überhaupt das ganze
prächtige Vehikel,
eine Madame Pompadour,
wie sie sagte, sie zog
Streichhölzer vor.

FAIRY TALES

At home in sugar-beet fields,
Sternickel,
a Wilhelmine murderer,
stony, how was it
with the bags of pepper,
the pursuers rubbing
their eyes, everywhere the
springs are failing, I want to
believe my Heine grandmother,
who was good at making things up
and knew her way with devil's thread,
looked out the godparents,
kept raw eggs in the cupboard, I
owe her some of my aversions,
for instance to
sunrises and sunsets,
and that whole
vehicular splendor,
a Madame Pompadour,
as she said, she preferred
safety matches.

RAUCHBIER

Brezelverkäufer und taubstumm,
meine Schlagzeilen,
die im Durchgang hocken
vor einem gemeinsamen Bier.

Ich starre auf ihre Gespräche,
ihr bescheidenes
und dauerhaftes Entsetzen,
meine Schlagzeilen,
meine Kennedys,
meine Chruschtschows.

RAUCHBIER

My headlines,
deaf-mute pretzel sellers
hunkered in the passage
sharing a beer.

I stare at their conversations,
their modest
and continual horror,
my headlines,
my Kennedys,
my Khruschevs.

ALTE POSTKARTEN

6

Erzähle mir was
aus den Katalogen,
und wo du lange warst,
von den Briefmarken im Bienenhaus,
den Großväterberufen
und vom Hufgeruch.
Ich zähl dir die Tropfen
auf den Zucker,
eine Primzahl,
und esse mit.

7

Paris,
das mich an mexikanische
Hüte erinnert,
Bänder
mit den Schritten der Lieblinge,
Auskünfte, Senfkörner.

8

Kraniche
gibt es keine bei uns.
Aber doch Frauen

OLD POSTCARDS

6

Tell me something
from the catalogs
and what kept you so long,
tell me about the stamps in the apiary,
ancestral professions
and the smell of horses' hooves.
I'll count out the drops
on your sugar lump,
a prime number,
and split it with you.

7

Paris,
which reminds me
of Mexican
hats, ribbons
with the tic-tac-toe of my darlings,
factoids, mustard seeds.

8

Cranes,
we have no cranes.
But women

und Wettläufe und
ein Gelächter zum Nachdenken,
alt wie
Renaissancetreppen
mit den Schritten der Zuchthäusler
hinab.

9

Wir gehören zu den letzten.
Links ein Höhlenkenner
fuhr gestern ab.
Das Eingekochte ist alle.
Ich dachte, auch gestern,
an die Ölkrüge der Kreuzfahrer,
mit übergeben an die Belagerer,
ehrenvoll,
an den Regen.

10

Warum der Kaffee
nicht getrunken wurde?
Wir saßen doch gut
in den Überschwemmungen,
hatten gemietete Kähne
zwischen den Boulevardbäumen.
Warum der Zucker
sich nicht löste?
Nichts kam zu Ende.
Zu erzählen sind
die Untertassen, eine
Charlotte, die kassierte, die
traurig durchnäßten Rüschen.

and foot races and
laughter that makes you think.
As old as
Renaissance staircases
that convicts
are busy descending.

9

We are among the last.
The speleologist on our left
finally went yesterday.
The preserves are all gone.
Yesterday, too, I found myself thinking
of the Crusaders and their jars of oil
handed over to the besiegers
with all ceremony,
and the rain.

10

Why was the coffee
not drunk?
We were sitting pretty
in the floods,
in rented boats
in among the avenue trees.
Why did the sugar
not dissolve?
Nothing was concluded.
All that remain to be spoken of
are the saucers,
the waitress—one Charlotte, supposedly—the
sodden ruches on her blouse.

11

Es geht,
es geht.
Aber wenn der Krieg vorbei ist,
fahren wir nach Minsk
und holen die Großmutter ab.

11

It's all right,
it's OK.
But once the war's over,
we'll go to Minsk
and pick up Gran.

NEUE POSTKARTEN

6

Die Katze erwartet auch hier
im Gras ihren Vogel.
Die Erdbeben hielten wir immer
für eine zufallende Tür.
Die Kinder werden grau.

7

Oh Jägergrün, Delphintage,
die Ahornböden
übersetzt in Gefühl.

Einverstanden,
so wollen wir lesen
die Anleitungen für Überlebende.

8

Palmyra
ist ein Zank um Trinkgelder,
Schwiegervater, Schwiegersohn,
die Oberfläche geht erdeinwärts,
Ablagerung von flüchtigem Hölderlin,
die richtigen Attribute,
weil er nicht da war,

NEW POSTCARDS

6

Here too, the cat expects
birds in the long grass.
We always mistook the earthquakes
for slamming doors.
The children are going rather gray.

7

Oh, British racing green, dolphin days,
the sycamore grounds
translated into feeling.

If you're agreed,
we'll read
the instruction manual for survivors.

8

Palmyra
is a squabble over tips,
father-in-law, son-in-law,
the surface is concave,
deposits of elusive Hölderlin,
correctly attributed
in his absence,

keine Deutungen,
die jemanden müde machen.

9

Ein kranker Schnee
und die in Tretbädern
leicht löslichen Patienten, –
hebt mich auf
für die vorletzte Sprechstunde,
wenn die endgültigen Winde
die langen Gedichte hersagen.

no interpretations
that would only make you tired.

9

A diseased snow
and the patients all too soluble
in footbaths—
put me down
for the penultimate consultation,
when the terminal winds
will recite long poems.

WEITGEREIST

Gleich hinter Vancouver
beginnt der Wald,
beginnt nichts,
beginnt, worüber wir fliegen.

Alles nördlich, wie du es liebst,
ein Salzkorn für die Waldläufer,
lederne Beutel, vielleicht
für Schwarzpulver, Gewürze, Tabak.

Was beginnt, geht sehr weit,
ein Rauch aus dem Böhmerwald,
ein Perspektiv, es gibt
wenig Menschen.

TRAVELING FAR

The forest begins
right behind Vancouver—
or nothing begins—
what we fly over begins.

All northerly, the way you like it,
a grain of salt for the woodsmen,
leather pouches, perhaps
for gunpowder, spices, baccy.

What begins goes on a long way,
smoke from the Bohemian woods,
a long view, not many
humans.

FORTSCHRITT

Entleert von Gedächtnis,
ich war fünf Glaskugeln,
ohne Laub, ohne Ausblicke:
Gestern wäre ein guter
Tag zum Sterben gewesen.
Heute beißen
den letzten die Hunde.

PROGRESS

Emptied of memory,
I was five marbles,
no leaves, no outlook.
Yesterday would have been
a good day on which to die,
because today the devil is taking
the hindmost.

HALB

Zwischen Kohlblättern
wächst die feierliche
Mohnstunde,
eine sandige Liebe,
die auswandert.
Geh! Auf den Regalen
gärt das Eingemachte,
wir können
Spinnweben pflücken
den Kanal entlang
und eine Tasche voll Sand
ungesehen wegtragen
aus der Baustelle,
wir könnten, wenn
die Zäune nicht wären,
querfeldein gehn bis
Amsterdam.

Aber
eine Schnecke geb ich dir mit,
die hält für lange.

HALF

There sprouts among cabbage
leaves the formal
poppy hour,
a sandy love
must emigrate.
On your way! Chutneys
are fermenting
on the shelves, we can
pluck spiders' webs
along the canal,
and fill our pockets
full of sand
from the building site
without being noticed;
we could, were it not
for the fences,
go cross country
as far as Amsterdam.

I'll give
you a snail for the road anyway,
that'll keep you going for a long time.

SATZZEICHEN

Sind gegangen,
sind gegangen wie Vögel, –
wer ging, wer flog,
Komma, Hühner,
Laufvögel, wer ging?

Sind gegangen,
sind geschwommen wie Hühner, –
siechenfarbig, die Bäche hinab,
wer ging, wer schwamm,
Fische, Fremdlinge,
Semikolon, wer ging?

Sind gegangen,
sind geflogen wie Fische,
wer ging, wer schwamm,
wer ist gestorben,
Hühner, unauffällige Kunden,
Fragezeichen,
Grenzgänger, wer ging?

PUNCTUATION MARKS

Are gone,
gone like the birds—
who walked, who flew,
comma, chickens,
waders, who's gone?

Are gone,
swum like the chickens—
liverish yellow, downstream,
who went, who swam,
fishes, furrin' fishes,
semicolon, who's gone?

Are gone,
flown like the fishes,
who went, who swam,
who died,
chickens, rum customers,
question mark,
walking gentleman, who's gone?

ZWEI

Beide Sizilien
und die Oliven schwarz und grün,
zwei Weinfarben,
zwei Vaterländer:
der Tag Gestern,
der Tag Morgen.
Draußen
fahren die Freunde
mit ihren Wirklichkeiten vorbei,
die Feinde
mit ihrem Einverständnis.

TWO

Both the Sicilies
and olives in black and green.
Two shades of wine,
two fatherlands:
the day called yester-
and the one called tomorrow.
Outside
my friends go by
with their several realities,
my enemies
with their common purpose.

BETT HÜTEN

Anginatage, blauer Schnee,
die Zeit versteckt
in Ausschnittbögen,
die Zeit ist blau, die Zeit ist Schnee,
und rote Ärmel, schwarzer Hut,
die Zeit ist eine gelbe Frau.

Anginatage, schweizerisch,
ist blau Devon,
schwarz Cambrium.
Commedia dell'arte Zeit,
Pantoffeln rot und rot Silur,
ein Plan von England gelb und Zeit.

Anginatage, blaues Kent,
die Zeit so gelb,
daß keiner sie erkennt,
ein schwarzer Zeigefinger
aus einem blauen Handschuh zeigt
die rote Mauer lang nachhause.

CONFINED TO BED

Angina days, blue snow,
time tucked away
in cut-out arches,
time is blue, time is snow,
red sleeves, black hat,
time is a yellow woman.

Angina days, Swiss,
blue Devon,
black Cambrium,
commedia dell'arte time,
slipper red and Silurian red,
wall map of England yellow and time.

Angina days, blue Kent,
time so yellow that none
can tell it, a black index finger
protrudes from a blue glove
and points you the way home
along the red wall.

SCHLUSS EINES KRIMINALROMANS

Ich behalte die Ratschläge:
Gin mit Tonic
und Vorsicht vor rohem Fisch,
keine Sorge!

Aber wer
bedenkt dich auf leeren Seiten,
wer gibt dir Namen
nach dem Impressum,
eine Feuerleiter,
ein Lieblingsgift?

Letzte Indizien
Rotweinflecken und Filzschuh.
Aber das Taxi ist bestellt,
mürrisch ticken die Zeilen.

Keine Hoffnung
auf römische Ziffern mehr,
keine halbe Seite mit dir,
kein geänderter Text,
keine Fingerabdrücke,
die deine sein könnten,
auf meinen Klinken.

THE END OF THE THRILLER

I'll remember the advice:
gin best with tonic
and steer clear of raw fish,
no worries!

But who
will think of you on empty pages,
who, after the note on the typeface,
will provide you with names,
a fire escape,
a pet poison?

Last traces
of claret stains and carpet slippers.
But the taxi is on its way,
the lines are ticking sullenly by.

No more hope
of Roman numerals,
not another half page with you,
no erratum slip,
no fingerprints
that might be yours
on my door handles.

ARMER SONNTAG

Armer Sonntag.
Eilige Verse auf
die Ölwolken der Autobusse,
auf Schneisen im Ahornlaub,
die abgekartete Schönheit.

Armer Sonntag,
blaugestreift, blaugepunktet,
die Schaukeln sind ausgehängt,
ins Museum der Tröstungen
geifert die Sonne ein
und zeigt auf den fröhlichen Staub.

Armer Sonntag,
Stunde der Prächtigen,
keine verstohlene Wollust
im toten Winkel,
alle Segel gehißt und mit starren
Brustwarzen in die Gesundheit.

POOR SUNDAY

Poor Sunday.
Hurried odes
to charabancs' petrol fumes,
sycamore glades,
hand-me-down beauties.

Poor Sunday,
blue stripes, blue spots,
the swings have been taken down,
in the museum of consolations
the drooling sun
points at the merry dust.

Poor Sunday,
hour of splendor,
no secret sin
behind the arras,
it's hoist all sails and nipples
erect and health here we come.

VERSPÄTUNG

Da bin ich gewesen
und da,
hätte auch
dorthin fahren können
oder zuhaus bleiben.
Ohne aus dem Hause zu gehen,
kannst du die Welt erkennen.
Laotse begegnete mir
früher als Marx.
Aber eine
gesellschaftliche Hieroglyphe
erreichte mich im linken Augenblick,
der rechte war schon vorbei.

DELAYED

I have been here
and here,
I could have
gone there too,
or stayed at home.
You can understand the world
without leaving home.
I encountered Lao Tse
before I met Marx.
But one
social hieroglyph
caught me at the left moment,
the right having already gone.

LANGE GEDICHTE

Normal

Sagt ihm,
er soll die Gabel links nehmen
und das Messer rechts.
Einarmig gilt nicht.

Vorsicht

Die Kastanien blühn.
Ich nehme es zur Kenntnis,
äußere mich aber echt dazu.

Zuversicht

In Saloniki
weiß ich einen, der mich liest,
und in Bad Nauheim.
Das sind schon zwei.

Stille Post für jedes Jahr

Ich sag dir den ersten Januar ins Ohr.
Sag ihn weiter, ich warte.

LONG POEMS

Normal

Tell him
to hold the fork in his left hand
and the knife in his right.
No accommodation for hemiplegics.

Cautious

The chestnuts are flowering.
I take cognizance of the fact,
but refrain from expressing an opinion.

Optimism

I have a reader
in Salonika,
and another in Bad Nauheim.
That makes two already.

Chinese Whispers for Each Year

I'll whisper the first of January in your ear.
Pass it on, I'll wait.

Zwischenbescheid für bedauernswerte Bäume

Akazien sind ohne Zeitbezug.
Akazien sind soziologisch unerheblich.
Akazien sind keine Akazien.

Papierzeit

Urkunden und Aquarelle
bewahrt der Erzvater
in Papprollen auf.
Künftigen Forschern ein Zufall,
ist es doch weise Voraussicht.

Beitrag zum Dantejahr

Chandler ist tot
und Dashiell Hammett.
Mir liegts nicht,
mich an das Böse schlechthin
zu halten und
Dante zu lesen.

Ode an die Natur

Wir haben unsern Verdacht
gegen Forelle, Winter
und Fallgeschwindigkeit.

Hart Crane

Mich überzeugen
die dünnen Schuhe, der
einfache Schritt über Stipendien
und Reling hinaus.

Provisional Downgrading of Certain Pitiable Trees

Acacias are not contemporary.
In sociological terms you can forget about acacias.
Acacias are not acacias.

Paper Age

The paterfamilias
keeps documents and watercolors
in cardboard rolls.
A lucky chance, in the view of future scholars,
but it was simple prudence.

Contribution to Dante's 700th Anniversary

Chandler is dead
and so is Dashiell Hammett.
I'd sooner not
binge
on evil
and read Dante.

Ode to Nature

We have our suspicions
on the subject of trout, winter,
and the speed of gravity.

Hart Crane

I am persuaded
by the thin soles, the
simple leap past government grants
and ship's rails.

Nach Seumes Papieren

From Seume's Papers (1972)

NÖRDLICHER SEUFZER

Links eine Straße zum Hafen. Nicht die Einwohner,
die Topographien sind entscheidend.
Der reformierte Kirchgang, rotweiße
Vermessungsstäbe bilden den Gottesbegriff.
Wie sich die Straße an einer zoologischen Handlung krümmt,
der Empfänger meiner Brieftelegramme könnte es Liebe nennen.

Man fährt nicht nach Venedig oder Kyoto. In Winkeln
spielt sich die Welt ab.

Nur keine Spuren hinterlassen.

NORTHERN SIGH

To the left, the road to the harbor. It's not the inhabitants
that matter so much as the topographical features.
The walk to the reformed church, red and white
surveyors' poles constitute the idea of God.
The way the road bends at a zoological negotiation—
the addressee of my lettergrams might be pleased to call it love.

People don't go to Kyoto or Venice. The world
happens in out of the way places.

Just mind you don't leave any tracks.

STADTRAND

Neubauten, ungeborene
Zimmer, nach zehn
bitte Stille im Sarg.

Das Salz, das Brot
den alleinstehenden Untermietern –
legs hin, die Schaben
sind geduldiger und
werden dir Trost
ins Weißbrot flüstern.

EDGE OF TOWN

New buildings, unborn
rooms, no more noise please
in your coffins after ten p.m.

Bread and salt
for the single occupancy tenants—
lay it down, the roaches
don't mind waiting and
will whisper condolences
into your white sliced.

PHILOLOGISCH

Ich dachte, ich schriebe für zwei.
Aber diese vertrackte
an Nadelholzzweigen hängende Schrift!

Man muß ein Examen machen
und die Kommilitonen
bleiben nach wenigen Doppelstunden aus.

Ich warte, weil der Lehrer mir leid tut.
Er hockt einsam inmitten seiner Schnalzlaute,
fröstelt in Gedanken an Schnee.

PHILOLOGICAL

I thought I was writing for two.
But that mazy script
looped over pine branches!

You have an exam to take
and your fellow students
are gone after just a few double-periods.

I'm waiting, because I feel sorry for the teacher.
He's hunkered there all alone among his labiodentals,
the thought of snow making him shiver.

NACH DEM ENDE DER BIOGRAPHIE

Vielleicht
hätte sich Trapezunt gelohnt.

Die schwarze Nordküste
mit Vokabeln der Volksbücher.

Er weiß es nicht,
wußte es nicht,
wird es nicht wissen.

AFTER SETTING DOWN THE BIOGRAPHY

Maybe
Trebizond would have been the place.

The bleak Northern shore
and a vocabulary out of nursery rhymes.

He doesn't know,
didn't know,
won't ever know.

OPTIK

Wenn das Auge schlechter wird,
geht man näher heran,
um die Freunde zu erkennen.

Setzt eine Brille auf,
benutzt Kontaktgläser
und bemerkt
ganz nahe
das Schwarze
unterm Fingernagel des Feindes.

OPTICS

As the eyesight gets weaker,
you take an extra step
to make out your friends.

Put on your glasses,
wear contact lenses
only to catch
a grandstand view
of the dirt
under your enemy's fingernails.

NAMEN

Namen mit i
oder Namen mit o,
umsonst versuche ich
mich an Konsonanten
zu erinnern.

Es rauscht vorbei
wie ein Telefonrauschen,
wie wie.
Ich horche angestrengt.
Viele Gespräche
im Jahre 1200,
sie betreffen mich,
aber die Aussprache ist anders,
ich habe Mühe.
Jemand mit a spricht
auf mich ein,
eine Art Händedruck,
den ich nicht erwidere,
ein Schluck Wein
eingetrocknet,
ein übriggebliebenes u,
ein vergebliches Ypsilon.

NAMES

Names with *i*
or names with *o*,
the effort to remember
consonants
seems beyond me.

It all hisses by
like the hiss on the phone,
like *like*.
I listen hard.
A lot of conversations
from the year 1200
concern me
but the pronunciation has changed,
which throws me off.
Someone with *a*
is addressing me now,
a particular pressure of the hand
that I don't return,
a sip of wine
baked dry,
a leftover *u*,
an unavailing *y*.

STEUERERKLÄRUNG

Verrottete Briefschaften (– inzwischen
Silbentrennung und Orthographie geändert –)
wir sammeln alles –

Telefonnummern
unsinnige Verabredungen,
Fliegenfüße.

Hier warten wir
auf den Mönch von Heisterbach,
auf sein rundes
Gesicht, das wir einmal hatten.
»Ach die Bilanz!« Er kommt atemlos.
Sind wir's?
Wir erkennen ihn nicht mehr.

TAX DECLARATION

Defunct correspondences (by now
hyphenation and spelling are different),
we collect everything—

telephone numbers,
hopeless appointments,
flies' feet.

Here we wait
for the monk of Heisterbach,
his round face
that was once ours.
"Oh, the balance!" His breathless approach.
Does he mean us?
We no longer recognize him.

AUGSBURG

Das träge Licht.

Ich badete gern mit Agnes Bernauer
aber sie ließ sich
in Straubing in einen Sack nähen.

Das Licht soll schnell sein,
aber es erreicht mich nicht.

So fand sie eine Möglichkeit
mir zu entfliehen,
träge wie Licht
schnell wie Licht.

AUGSBURG

The sluggish light.

I used to like going swimming with Agnes Bernauer
but she had herself sewn into a sack
in Straubing.

Light is supposed to be fast,
but it doesn't reach me.

So she found a possibility
to escape from me –
sluggish as light,
fast as light.

NACH SEUMES PAPIEREN

Ob die ehrlichen Huronen
den steigenden Luftdruck
ausgleichen konnten –
sie sind mir nie begegnet.
Ich denke an Fähigkeiten
weit über die Ehrlichkeit.

Dabei könnte sie genug sein
als Trost, als Untrost,
als Wetterbeobachtung,
ein Reisesouvenir
und Erleichterung
des gichtigen Sterbens.

FROM SEUME'S PAPERS

Whether the honest Hurons
were able to
compensate for the rising air pressure—
I never met them.
I'm thinking about qualities
far beyond honesty.

But it might do:
as comfort, as discomfort,
as meteorological observation,
as souvenir of foreign parts,
as relief against
a gouty death.

SPÄTER

Erfahrungen abdrehen
und ungehemmt
zählen bis
93, auch weiter.

Jedenfalls
für die Silvesternacht
1999
bin ich verabredet.
Weiter im Gebirge, auf
einem Kanapee,
freue mich, man hat
wenig Abwechslung.

LATER

Disregard prudence
and count
freely
to 93 and beyond.

At any rate
I have an engagement
for New Year's Eve,
1999.
Higher up the mountain,
on a chaise longue, I'm pleased,
don't encounter much
in the way of variety.

from Uncollected Poems and

Poems from Radio Plays

DER REGEN IN ELTVILLE

Der Regen in Eltville,
der gleiche Regen wie anderswo,
Wassertropfen mit Beimengung von Staub,
einmal verdunstet aus Gewässern, die mir unbekannt sind,
der gleiche Regen und doch ein andrer, wie ich ihn trommeln höre:
Er ist für mich.

Während jenseits der Wand das Fensterblech schallt,
nimmt jemand zwanzig Tabletten Veronal,
vor der Zärtlichkeit eines Blickes bebt mir das Herz,
und es bleiben auch die mageren Arme meiner Neffen aus Berlin.

Hier sitze ich unter dem Schutze des Dachs
und ich kann einen Mantel anziehen, wenn ich hinausgehe,
aber er traf mich längst, er wird mich ertränken,
Regen des Wahnsinns, der Liebe, Armutsregen,
der Regen in Eltville.

THE RAIN IN ELTVILLE

The rain in Eltville,
same rain as everywhere else,
drops of water mingled with dust
evaporated from God knows what reservoir,
the same rain but different, as I listen to its drumming:
this rain is for me.

While the tin windowsill echoes the other side of the wall,
someone is taking twenty veronal,
my heart shakes at the tenderness in someone's eyes,
and there are always the scrawny arms of my nephews in Berlin.

I sit here in the lee of the roof
and I can put on a coat to go outside,
but it's hit me long ago, it will drown me,
the rain of madness, of love, the rain of poverty,
the rain in Eltville.

PLÄNE

Mit dem Rücken
an meine Pläne gelehnt,
über mürrisches Pflaster,
eingedenk der Ermordeten,
der unlesbaren Knotenschnüre,
der Sternwarten
und der tauben Stellen des Fleisches,
der Maya und der Brachvögel
abwandernd,
und aufgegeben die Schnalzlaute
afrikanischer Sprachen.

PLANS

Propping my back
against my plans
on morose plasterboard;
remaining mindful of the victims,
the illegible knotted ropes,
the observatories,
and the insentient parts of flesh,
drifting onto Mayas
curlews,
and gradually neglecting
the clicks of Xhosa.

VORWINTER

Ruh dich lange aus
von der warmen Milch,
dem frisch gefallenen Schnee.
Die Drucksachen warten nicht länger.

Ein Grasgelände, von Katzengräbern durchsetzt.
Meine Tochter wartet auf den Winter,
sie wächst aus den Schischuhen.
Mir wird das Postfach zu groß.

Morgen nehme ich Klavierunterricht,
es ist nie zu spät.
Der fröhliche Landmann
fährt eine Spur in den Schnee.

EARLY WINTER

Take a rest
after your hot milk
and the fresh snowfall.
There's printed matter that needs your attention.

Pastureland, riddled with cats' graves.
My little girl is waiting for winter,
she is growing out of her skis.
My postbox is too big for my needs.

Tomorrow I will start taking piano lessons,
they say it's never too late.
The jolly countryman
is making tracks in the snow.

ALTER DEZEMBER

Ein
unwiderbringlicher Schneefall,
vorgeschichtliche Gräber.

OLD DECEMBER

An
irreparable snowfall,
prehistoric graves.

NOMADEN

Zeit für mich,
das Gebirge abzukarren.
Ich hätte das Land gern flach.

Ich dachte:
Plattdeutsche Sätze,
Nomaden,
die an ihren teppichfreien
Tagen kommen, um mich
herumgehen und flüstern
aus dem Koran, plattdeutsch.

Wer kommt, hat sich
in meine Irrtümer verlaufen,
geht ohne Anruf davon.

NOMADS

Time for me
to remove the mountains.
I prefer the land flat.

I thought:
Platt German sentences,
nomads,
coming on their carpet-free days,
to walk around me and
whisper out of the Koran
in Platt German.

Whoever comes
has become enmeshed in my errors,
leaves without calling.

FREUND UND HORAZLESER

Sag mir nicht wieder: Horaz
und sterben lernen.
Keiner hat es gelernt,
es fiel sie nur an
wie die Geburt.

FRIEND AND READER OF HORACE

Please don't talk to me again about Horace
and learning to die.
No one learned that,
it just befell them,
a bit like being born.

AUS: TRÄUME

Ich beneide sie alle, die vergessen können,
die sich beruhigt schlafen legen und keine Träume haben.
Ich beneide mich selbst um die Augenblicke blinder Zufriedenheit
erreichtes Urlaubsziel, Nordseebad, Notre Dame,
roter Burgunder im Glas und der Tag des Gehaltsempfangs.
Im Grunde aber meine ich, daß auch das gute Gewissen nicht
    ausreicht,
und ich zweifle an der Güte des Schlafes, in dem wir uns alle
    wiegen.
Es gibt kein reines Glück mehr (– gab es das jemals? –),
und ich möchte den einen oder andern Schläfer aufwecken können
und ihm sagen, es ist gut so.
Fuhrest auch du einmal aus den Armen der Liebe auf,
weil ein Schrei dein Ohr traf, jener Schrei,
den unaufhörlich die Erde ausschreit und den du
für Geräusch des Regens sonst halten magst oder das Rauschen des
    Winds.
Sieh, was es gibt: Gefängnis und Folterung,
Blindheit und Lähmung, Tod in vieler Gestalt,
den körperlosen Schmerz und die Angst, die das Leben meint.
Die Seufzer aus vielen Mündern sammelt die Erde,
und in den Augen der Menschen, die du liebst, wohnt die
    Bestürzung.
Alles, was geschieht, geht dich an.

FROM: DREAMS

I envy all those who are capable of forgetting,
who calmly go off into dreamless sleep.
I even envy myself for odd moments of blind contentment,
reaching a vacation destination, whether North Sea spa or Notre
    Dame,
or with a nice drop of Burgundy on pay day.
But basically I'm of the view that even a clear conscience is not
    sufficient,
and I doubt the quality of the sleep in which we all rock ourselves.
There is no such thing as pure happiness any more (was there
    ever?),
and I should like to rouse this or that sleeper,
and say, there, that's enough.
Where you once leaped up out of the arms of love
because a scream reached your ear, the scream
that the earth utters incessantly, which you
take to be the patter of raindrops or the soughing of wind.
Look at what's happening: prison and torture,
blindness and amputation, death in many guises,
disembodied pain and dread that stands in for life.
The earth collects up the groans from many mouths,
and the expressions of people you love are full of horror.
Everything that happens concerns you.

Denke daran, dass der Mensch des Menschen Feind ist
und daß er sinnt auf Vernichtung.
Denke daran immer, denke daran jetzt,
während eines Augenblicks im April,
unter diesem verhangenen Himmel,
während du das Wachstum als ein feines Knistern zu hören glaubst,
die Mägde Disteln stechen
unter dem Lerchenlied,
auch in diesem Augenblick denke daran!

Während du den Wein schmeckst in den Kellern von Randersacker
oder Orangen pflückst in den Gärten von Alicante,
während du einschläfst im Hotel Miramar nahe dem Strand von
    Taormina,
oder am Allerseelentage eine Kerze entzündest auf dem Friedhof in
    Feuchtwangen,
während du als Fischer das Netz aufholst über der Doggerbank,
oder in Detroit eine Schraube vom Fließband nimmst,
während du Pflanzen setzt in den Reis-Terrassen von Szetschuan,
auf dem Maultier über die Anden reitest, –
denke daran!

Denke daran, wenn eine Hand dich zärtlich berührt,
denke daran in der Umarmung deiner Frau,
denke daran beim Lachen deines Kindes!

Denke daran, daß nach den großen Zerstörungen
jedermann beweisen wird, daß er unschuldig war.

Denke daran:
Nirgendwo auf der Landkarte liegt Korea und Bikini,
aber in deinem Herzen.
Denke daran, daß du schuld bist an allem Entsetzlichen,
Das sich fern von dir abspielt –

◆

Remember that the enemy of man is man,
and that he is set on annihilation.
Remember it always, but remember it in particular now,
at this moment in April
under a cloudy sky
in which you think you can hear the faint clicking sound of things
    growing,
while the maids are weeding thistles
under a canopy of lark song,
think of it even now!

While you swill the wine in your mouth in the cellars of
    Randersacker,
or pick oranges in the gardens of Alicante,
while you go off to sleep in the Hotel Miramar by the strand at
    Taormina,
or while lighting a candle on All Souls' Day in the cemetery at
    Feuchtwangen,
while, a fisherman now, you haul in your nets over the Dogger Bank,
or pick a spare part from a conveyor belt in Detroit,
while you set seedlings in the rice terraces of Sichaun,
or sit astride a mule crossing the Andes—
think of it!

Remember when a hand softly caresses you,
remember it in bed with your wife,
remember it when you hear the laughter of your son!

Remember that, following the great destructions,
everyone will provide an alibi for himself to prove he had no part in
    them.

Remember:
Korea and Bikini do not exist on any map,
but in your heart.
Remember that you are personally to blame for all the horror
that is taking place far away—

In der Stunde X werde ich dennoch denken, dass die Erde schön
      war.
Ich werde an die Freunde denken, an die Güte, die ein häßliches
      Gesicht schön macht,
an die Liebe, die die Augen verzaubert.
Ich werde an den Hund denken, meinen Spielgefährten, als ich ein
      Kind war,
an die blauen Lupinen der Samlandküste während eines
      Ferienbesuchs,
ich werde noch einmal die langen Schatten der Tannen sehn auf der
      Bauernschmied-Alm
und mit Emmy Gruber auf den Gederer gehn,
ich werde mich erinnern an die Vogelzüge über dem Flugplatz von
      Märkisch-Friedland,
an den Geruch des Bierkellers im Gasthaus zum Hirschen, das
      meinem Großvater gehörte,
an Holunder, Raps und Mohn, flüchtig gesehen von einem
      Zugfenster aus,
an das Erröten der vierzehnjährigen Gabriele Dembitza,
an die roten und grünen Lichter eines Flugzeugs, das unter dem
      Sternbild der Cassiopeia dahinflog,
an den Tanz unter den Lampions des Quatorze Juillet,
an den Duft von Obst morgens an den Verkaufsständen vorm
      Schloß in Celle,
ich werde denken an den Herzschlag der Eidechse, die mich
      erblickt hat,
und an ein Gedicht im »Westöstlichen Diwan«, das mich tröstete.

At the given hour, I will nonetheless think that the world was
     beautiful.
I will think of friends, of the kindness that can beautify an ugly face,
of love that causes the eyes to light up.
I will think of the dog, my playmate when I was a boy,
of the blue lupins on the coast of East Prussia where I once went on
     holiday.
I will revisit the long shadows of the firs on the Bauernschmied
     meadow,
and climb the Gederer once more with Emmy Gruber,
I will remember the flights of migrating birds over the airfield at
     Märkisch-Friedland,
and the smell of the beer cellar of the Inn zum Hirschen which
     belonged to my grandfather,
of elderflower, rapeseed and poppy, glimpsed from the window of a
     train,
of the blush on the face of the fourteen year old Gabriele Dembitza,
of the red and green lights of an airplane flying under the
     constellation of Cassiopeia,
of dancing under paper lanterns on Bastille Day,
the smell of fruit in the morning on the stands in front of the castle
     at Celle,
I will think of the quivering heart of the lizard that spotted me,
and a poem in Goethe's "West-East Divan" that gave me comfort.

＊

Es gibt Wegweiser an den Strassen,
leicht erkennbare Flußläufe,
Aussichtsgerüste an erhöhten Punkten,
Landkarten, auf denen die Seen blau eingezeichnet sind
und die Wälder grün,
– es ist leicht, sich zurechtzufinden auf der Erde.

Aber du, der du neben mir gehst, wie verborgen
ist mir die Landschaft deines Herzens!
Tappend im Nebel überkommt mich oft Furcht
vorm Dickicht und vorm verborgenen Abgrund.
Ich weiß, du willst nicht, daß man deine Gedanken durchwandre,
irreführen soll das Echo deiner Worte,
– Straßen, die kein Ziel haben,
ein Gebiet ohne Ausweg, verfallne Markierung.
Jedes Jahrhundert gibt uns neue Dinge zu verbergen,
ein Gelände, überwachsen dem neugierigen Auge der Liebe,
zugedeckt von Einsamkeit, dem immer dichteren Laub.

There are road signs,
and easily discernable river courses,
lookout points in elevated positions,
maps where the lakes are in blue and the forests in green—
it's easy to find one's way around in the world.

But you, companion at my side, how hidden from me
is the landscape of your heart!
Feeling my way in the fog, I am often overcome with fear
of the thickets and the hidden precipice.
I know you don't like your thoughts to be traced,
the echo of your words is intended to mislead—
roads going nowhere,
pathless terrain, lapsed signage.
Each century provides us with new things to conceal,
a territory that offers no purchase to the curious eye of affection,
overgrown with loneliness, its ever denser leaves.

♦

Wacht auf, denn eure Träume sind schlecht!
Bleibt wach, weil das Entsetzliche näher kommt.

Auch zu dir kommt es, der weit entfernt wohnt von den Stätten wo
    Blut vergossen wird,
auch zu dir und deinem Nachmittagsschlaf,
worin du ungern gestört wirst.
Wenn es heute nicht kommt, kommt es morgen,
aber sei gewiß.
»Oh, angenehmer Schlaf
auf den Kissen mit roten Blumen,
einem Weihnachtsgeschenk von Anita, woran sie drei Wochen
    gestickt hat,
oh, angenehmer Schlaf,
wenn der Braten fett war und das Gemüse zart.
Man denkt im Einschlummern an die Wochenschau von gestern
    abend:
Osterlämmer, erwachende Natur, Eröffnung der Spielbank in
    Baden-Baden,
Cambridge siegte gegen Oxford mit zweieinhalb Längen, –
das genügt, das Gehirn zu beschäftigen.

Oh, dieses weiche Kissen, Daunen aus erster Wahl!
Auf ihm vergißt man das Ärgerliche der Welt, jene Nachricht zum
    Beispiel:
Die wegen Abtreibung Angeklagte sagte zu ihrer Verteidigung:
Die Frau, Mutter von sieben Kindern, kam zu mir mit einem
    Säugling,
für den sie keine Windeln hatte und der
in Zeitungspapier gewickelt war.
Nun, das sind Angelegenheiten des Gerichtes, nicht unsre.
Man kann dagegen nichts tun, wenn einer etwas härter liegt als der
    andere,
Und was kommen mag, unsere Enkel mögen es ausfechten.«

◆

Wake up, your dreams are bad!
Stay awake, the nightmarishness is coming ever nearer.

To you too it is coming, though you live far from the places of
     bloodshed,
even to you and your sacrosanct
afternoon nap.
If not today, then tomorrow,
but it will certainly come.
"Oh, pleasant sleep
on the cushions embroidered with red flowers,
Anita's Christmas present to you, she sat over the stitching for all of
     three weeks,
oh, pleasant sleep,
following the juicy roast and the sprouts boiled to pulp.
As you drift off you think of yesterday's Fox Evening News:
frolicsome Easter lambs, the stirrings of nature, the opening of the
     new casino in Baden-Baden,
with their new Australian coach, the Light Blues pip the Dark Blues
by two and a half lengths in the Varsity Race—
more than enough there to occupy the brain.

Oh the soft cushion, the first-class goose down!
Lying on it, you forget the irritations of the world, this item for
     instance:
the doctor accused of procuring an abortion said in his defense:
"The woman had seven children already, and she came to me with
     her youngest
swaddled in newspaper
because she was unable to afford diapers.
Well, these are the court's affairs, not ours.
There's nothing to be done if A has a cushier time of it than B,
and, whatever happens, our grandchildren can sort it out."

»Ah, du schläfst schon? Wache gut auf, mein Freund!
Schon läuft der Strom in den Umzäunungen, und die Posten sind
  aufgestellt.«

Nein, schlaft nicht, während die Ordner der Welt geschäftig sind!
Seid mißtrauisch gegen ihre Macht, die sie vorgeben für euch
  erwerben zu müssen!
Wacht darüber, daß eure Herzen nicht leer sind, wenn mit der
Leere eurer Herzen gerechnet wird!
Tut das Unnütze, singt die Lieder, die man aus eurem Mund nicht
  erwartet!
Seid unbequem, seid Sand, nicht das Öl im Getriebe der Welt!

"Ah, asleep already? A pleasant waking then, friend!
The current is already live in the wire kraal, and the sentries have
  been posted."

No, don't sleep while the governors of the world are busy!
Be suspicious of the power they claim to have to acquire on your
  behalf!
Stay awake to be sure that your hearts are not empty, when others
  calculate on the emptiness of your hearts!
Do what is unhelpful, sing songs from out of your mouths that go
  against expectation!
Be ornery, be as sand, not oil in the thirsty machinery of the world!

HÄNDEL

Er liebte den Luxus und fraß wie ein Schwein.
Aber der Diener, der die Schokolade ans Bett brachte,
fand ihn in Tränen.
Die Vergänglichkeit begegnete ihm als Musik.

HANDEL

He loved luxury and ate like a pig.
But the servant who brought him his chocolate in bed
found him in floods of tears.
Mortality proposed itself to him in the form of music.

NAPOLEON DENKT AN JOSEPHINE

Daß sie mir keinen Sohn gebar,
erschien mir einst unerträglich.
Auf Sankt Helena sehen die Dinge sich anders an.
Ich vertauschte sie mit einer langweiligen Person,
die ich vergessen habe.
Ah Josephine! Wie herrlich war sie, wenn sie ins Bett stieg!

NAPOLEON REMEMBERS JOSEPHINE

The fact that she never presented me with a son
at one time would have seemed unpardonable to me.
On St. Helena I view things differently.
I got her mixed up once with some other ghastly woman
I had quite forgotten.
But Josephine! How majestic she used to be, coming to bed!

LANGE GEDICHTE

Zugetan den
Hühneraugenoperateuren,
heimlich saufenden
Nachtschwestern,
Leichenwäschern, Abortfrauen.

Abgeneigt
prominenten Friseuren,
Fürstenhochzeiten,
Brechtplatten,
Realistischer Literatur.

LONG POEMS

In favor of
podiatrists,
tippling
night nurses,
corpse washers, bathroom attendants.

Against
celebrity hairdressers,
society weddings,
Brecht LPs,
realistic literature.

DIE VORIGE WOCHE

Mittwoch. Die Kastanien beeilen sich.
Kein Zeitwort,
den Donnerstag zu verhindern.

Mein Vater wäre jetzt hundert.
Die Nachkommen haben sich abgefunden,
schleifen Kastaniensäcke
an die Hauswand, – sie werden
vergessen wie Symmetrien.

Man holt uns überall ein.

In Delhi, wenn man stirbt,
kann man nicht fallen.

LAST WEEK

Wednesday. The chestnuts are in a rush.
No verb
can prevent Thursday.

My father would be a hundred now.
His heirs have come to an accommodation,
are lugging sacks of chestnuts
against the wall—where they are
forgotten like symmetries.

Everywhere we are being overtaken.

In Delhi, if a man dies,
he is unable to drop.

UND

Nebel Nebel Nebel
und in den Ohren
Haare, eine
unverbindliche
Freundlichkeit
und
und
Rajissas süßes Gelächter.

Was zusammengehört,
eine Erfahrung,
was mit und zusammengehört
nur mit und,
keine Begründungen.

Das wird anhalten
wenn mir das und nicht
mit den andern Wörtern entfällt.
Es reicht, es reicht, danke, es reicht.

AND

Fog fog fog,
hair
in my ears, a
noncommittal
friendliness
and
and
and Raissa's sweet laugh.

Experience tells
what belongs with what,
what belongs with *and*,
only with *and*,
no rationale.

It will last
so long as the *and* doesn't
slip my mind like the other words.
It's enough, thanks, it's plenty.

LANDGASTHOF

Sichtbar wächst
den Bäumen der Bart.
25 Watt-Hotels
und in den Treppengeländern
Elektrizität.

Es muß ein Bild geben,
man findet es nicht,
nur Einzelheiten summiert
zu psychischer Blindheit.

Der Dickdarm
ist der Mörder des Menschen,
er ruht sich aus,
gehört nicht ins Bild,
aber er kennt alle Daten
für bärtige Hotels –
viel Zeit, blinde Zeit.

RUSTIC HOTEL

The trees grow beards
before your very eyes.
25 watt hotels
and you get a shock
from the banisters.

There must be an image,
I can't find it,
only details that taken together
make spiritual obtuseness.

The bowel
is the murderer of man,
it is at rest,
keeps out of the picture,
but it knows all there is to be known
about the bearded hotels—
so much time, obtuse time.

KLINIKFARBEN

Dem Graugrün kann man
auf die Spur kommen,
dem Wandanstrich, der Tapete,
erwacht erfährst du es gleich,
wenn du die Frage noch hast,
versteck sie in einer Zahnlücke,
daß die grasgrünen Mädchen
sie nicht mitnehmen können
in grasgrünen Mützen, Mundbinden,
grasgrünen Wörtern.

HOSPITAL COLORS

It's possible to
get on the case of that gray green,
the walls, the paper,
the second you come round you will experience it;
if you still have a question,
bite it back,
so that the grass green girls
can't take it away with them
in their grass green bonnets, surgical masks,
their grassgreen words.

VOM GLÜCK

Vom Glück
bleiben zwei Papageien übrig,
der Münzfernsprecher.
Die Sätze wird jemand fortsetzen,
der recht hat
und die passenden Münzen.
Mich verläßt mein Gedächtnis,
ich vergesse den eigenen Namen.
Das Grau des Papageiengefieders
ist schwer zu benennen.

OF HAPPINESS

Two parrots are what remain
of happiness,
the call box.
The sentences will be completed
by someone who has right on his side
and the correct change.
My memory is abandoning me,
I forget my own name.
The gray of parrot feathers
eludes description.